My Big Prayer Book

First steps in talking with God

Maggie Barfield

My Big Prayer Book

My name

_____

Given by

_____

on

_____

© Maggie Barfield 1997, 2009
This edition first published 2010
ISBN 978 1 84427 530 4

Some material previously published in *Talking to God*.

Scripture Union
207–209 Queensway, Bletchley, Milton Keynes, MK2 2EB
Email: info@scriptureunion.org.uk
Website: www.scriptureunion.org.uk

Scripture Union Australia
Locked Bag 2, Central Coast Business Centre, NSW 2252
Website: www.scriptureunion.org.au

Scripture Union USA
PO Box 987, Valley Forge, PA 19482
Website: www.scriptureunion.org

British Library Cataloguing-in-Publication Data
A catalogue record of this book is available from the
British Library.

Printed and bound in Hong Kong by 1010 Printing
International Ltd

Cover and internal design: kwgraphicdesign

Photography: Steve Shipman
Art direction: Mark Carpenter
Photographs taken at Goodmayes Church

Scripture Union is an international charity working with
churches in more than 130 countries, providing resources
to bring the good news of Jesus Christ to children, young
people and families and to encourage them to develop
spiritually through the Bible and prayer.

As well as our network of volunteers, staff and associates
who run holidays, church-based events and school Christian
groups, we produce a wide range of publications and
support those who use our resources through training
programmes.

What's inside

First steps in talking with God

Kim had been hearing about children without clean drinking water. At bedtime, she prayed, without prompting: 'Dear Jesus, thank you for water. Please help children who have dirty water to have clean water and not get ill. Amen.' What else needed to be said?!

Prayer is simply another name for communicating with God. Any method that your child can use to communicate can be used for prayer. Don't be afraid that they won't know what to say or do. Given a little time, encouragement and experience, children can be amazing in their prayers. They get straight to the point and expect God to answer! And their prayers are of value to God: their praises are powerful (Psalm 8:2); and they recognise who Jesus is when others reject him (Matthew 21:15,16).

Children simply chat to God. They pray naturally and easily, when set the example. The key principle is to keep it short and simple. Create an environment where children learn to delight, spontaneously, in spending time with God, rather than long devotional sessions, which are beyond the young child's level of concentration.

As first steps in praying, young children are likely to bring their 'pleases' and 'thank yous' to God. We can model this to them, through praying together and sharing our own experiences of answered prayer. Children are usually over 4 years old before they begin to understand that we need to pray 'sorry' prayers – to tell Jesus that we are sad when we have done something wrong. The prayers in this book span all these areas and also include 'chatty' prayers, using childlike words to express everyday thoughts and experiences.

Let prayer be a natural part of your child's daily life, both talking and listening to God. And you may find that praying with your child helps your own prayer life too!

Praising prayers

To help children discover what it means to 'praise' God, explain that it means saying good things about him. Use these prayers to prompt more good sayings!

God does

Who makes us happy
together? God does.
Who makes us laugh
together? God does.
Who helps us care for
each other? God does.
Who helps us have fun
together?
God does.
Thank you,
Father God!

All the people!

Father God, it's fantastic to know
that of all the people in this street,
all the people in this town,
all the people in this country,
all the people in this continent,
all the people in this hemisphere,
all the people in this world,
you love and care for me!

God is good

God is good to me,
God is good to me,
he helps me care,
he helps me share,
God is good to me.

God is good to me,
God is good to me,
he helps me know,
he helps me show,
God is good to me.

God is good to me,
God is good to me,
he's always there,
he hears my prayer,
God is good to me.

My friend, Jesus

Hello Jesus!
I'm going to jump up and down
and shout out loud
because you're my friend, Jesus.
I'm going to listen and pray,
all through the day,
because I'm your friend, too.

Love is

Love is...

cuddly like a bedtime toy.

Love is...

snuggly like a fluffy kitten.

Love is...

warm like a bowl of soup.

Love is...

gentle like people who care for me.

Love is...

you, Jesus.

God made me

God made the land,
   the sky and the sea,
God made the plants,
   the flowers and the trees,
God made the animals,
   the birds and the bees,
and the best thing of all is that –
   God made me!

How great you are

Father God, how great you are!
From the sky, God sends rain on the hills.
Father God, how great you are!
God makes grass to grow for the cattle,
and plants for people to use.
Father God, how great you are!
God gives us good food to eat,
to make us happy and strong.
Father God, how great you are!

You never forget me

I don't know where I left my socks,
I've lost my other shoe,
I don't know what I had to take,
or what I had to do.
I'm thinking of so many things,
but this one thing is true –
I know you never forget me
and I remember you.

I've put my pencils somewhere,
and I really ought to know,
it's like this every morning,
when it comes to,
"Time to go!"
I'm thinking of so
many things,
but this,
I know is true –
I know you never
forget me
and I remember you.

You made them all

Father God, you made the light,
thank you for all you made.
Father God, you made the sky,
thank you for all you made.
You made the sun, you made the moon,
you made the stars that shine.
Father God, you made them all –
thank you for all you made.

Water!

Water is such sploshy stuff:
in the puddles (splat splat),
in the bath (splash splash),
in the pool (splush splush),
in the stream (splish splish),
in the tap (swish swish),
in my mouth (slurp slurp).
Thank you, God, for water!

You love us

Dear God,
your world is full of people
who are very much like me.
Some move around in wheelchairs,
some deaf, some cannot see.
Each one of us is special
for you know us each by name.
Each one of us is precious
for you love us each the same.

My very special friend

I'm writing on a card,
drawing kisses at the end.
It's a very special message,
to a very special friend.

When I want to talk to Jesus,
I don't need a card to send.
He is always here to hear me,
he's my very special friend.

God's world

There's a rainbow, packed with colours,
that looks brilliant.
Well done, God!

There's a fast plane zooming over,
shining, glistening.
Thank you, God!

Your world,
   My world,
      World of wonder –
WHAT A GREAT WORLD!
THANK YOU GOD!

Tall and small

Everything is big — except me!
Grown ups are tall,

trees are

taller,

skyscrapers are

tallest.

Jesus, I'm glad you
were once a child.
You know what
it's like to be
small,

smaller,

smallest.

My own prayers

What do you want to say to God?
Say it here.

Thanking
prayers

Saying 'thank you' to God is often the way a child begins their relationship with him. They will happily thank him for anything and everything!

A new day

Hello God, it's a new day,
a "wonder what I'll do" day,
a "have a happy day" day,
a "fun and games and play" day,
a "THANK YOU FOR TODAY" day.

Please be with me, today.

My new shoes

Father God,
look at my new shoes!
Long shoes for my long feet,
wide shoes for my wide feet,
two shoes for my two feet!
Thank you, God, for my new shoes!

Noises!

Thank you, God, for great big noises:
  banging drums, clanging cymbals.
Thank you, God, for little noises:
  squeaking mice, trickling water.
Thank you, God, for ears to hear
  all the sounds around me.

Thank you, God, for gentle noises:
  Mummy singing, kittens purring.
Thank you, God, for funny noises:
  Daddy snoring, children laughing.
Thank you, God, for ears
  to hear all the sounds
    around me.

My food and drink

Here's my plate of food to eat,
and my drink to stop my thirst.
It looks so tasty, I want to start,
but I'm going to say "thank you" first.

Thank you, God!

Being well

Thank you for the scientists
who use their clever skills
to make special medicines
to stop me being ill.

Thank you for the doctor
who gives my skin a prick
to give me my injection
to stop me getting sick.

Always

Father God,
You're always with me –
when I'm awake,
when I'm asleep,
when I'm at home,
when I go out,
when I'm busy,
when I'm quiet,
all the time,
all day long.
You're always with me!
Thank you, God.

Safe with God

Dear God,
when I am feeling sad,
thank you for keeping me safe.
When I am feeling all alone,
thank you for keeping me safe.
When I am feeling scared,
thank you for keeping me safe,
ALWAYS.

I'm happy being me!

Thank you, God, for running, jumping,
hopping, dancing, friends to play.
Thank you, God, for watching, looking,
learning, playing every day.
   I'm happy being me!

Thank you, God, for laughing, smiling,
speaking, humming, singing out.
Thank you, God, for whispers, giggles,
chatting, calling, great big shouts.
   I'm happy being me!

Thank you, God, for helping,
      caring,
cuddles when I'm feeling sad.
Thank you, God, for loving,
      sharing:
being special makes me glad.
   I'm happy being me!

You are with us

Thank you that you are with us every day.
You are with us when we go on holiday.
You are with us when we stay at home.
You are with us when we are together
and when we are alone.

People I love

Thank you, God, for my dad.
When I'm sad, he makes me smile.
When I'm scared, he holds my hand.
When I'm sorry, he gives me a hug.
When it all goes wrong,
Dad puts things right.
I love him.

Thank you, God,
for my mum.
When I'm sad,
she makes me smile.
When I'm scared,
she holds my hand.
When I'm sorry, she gives me a hug.
When it all goes wrong,
Mum puts things right.
I love her.

Change the words of this prayer to fit your child's experience of family relationships.

Good friends

Lord Jesus,
thank you for all my friends.
Friends at home.
Friends at nursery (school).
Friends at church.
Help me to be good friends with them.

Lord Jesus,
Thank you for being my friend.
You're my friend at home.
You're my friend at nursery (school).
You're my friend at church.
Help me to be good friends with you.

Tonight

Please, Jesus,
stay with me tonight.
I want to know you're near.
When bad dreams scare me
    in the night,
it's good to know you're here!

My home

Here is my home.
Thank you, God.

Here's where I laugh,
here's where I eat,
here's where I play,
here's where I sleep.
Here is my home.
Thank you, God.

Here's where I think,
here's where I love,
here's where I share,
here's where I belong,
here is my home.
Thank you, God.

My family

I love them
and they love me.
Thank you for
my family.

At the dentist's

The dentist's room's a spaceship
all silver, bright and clean.
The dentist's chair goes flying
and the Space Captain is ME!

The nurse and dentist are my crew,
as I open my mouth wide.
The dentist's mirror curves around
to help her check inside.

Thank you that my dentist helps
my teeth keep strong and white.
Please help me learn to clean my teeth
each morning and each night.

All day long

I wake up in the
morning and say,
"THANK YOU, GOD!
It's a fresh new day,
today."

At mealtimes I say,
"THANK YOU, GOD,
for all my food,
today."

At bedtime I say,
"THANK YOU, GOD,
for all I've done,
today."

THANK YOU, GOD!
THANK YOU, GOD!
THANK YOU, GOD!
HURRAY!

Any time
prayers

Young children do not need a reason to talk with God. They are happy simply chatting with him about their feelings, what they have been doing and anything that springs to mind at the time.

The only one!

Two eyes,
two ears,
one mouth,
one nose,
ten waggly fingers,
ten wriggly toes,
two arms,
two legs,
one back,
one tum –
that makes me
THE ONLY ONE!!!

Thank you, God,
that you made me the only one!

You are there

Dear Father, you are with me
when I'm happy or sad.
You know just how I'm feeling,
if I'm grumpy or glad.
I know you always love me
and I know that you care,
and it makes me feel better
just to know you are there.

I don't want to go

I don't want to go.
It will all be new and strange
and I won't know anybody there.

Does everyone else feel the same?
They won't know me, either.
Perhaps I could say "hello"...
perhaps we'll make friends...
please be with me, God.

Messy play

My thumbs are stuck with sticky tape,
my finger's in the glue,
I'm in a gooey, painty mess.
What have I made?
It's hard to guess!
It will take ages
    to get clean —
but, Lord,
    you know what
    fun it's been.

41

God is there

When I fall and hurt
    my elbow,
when I have a horrid
    dream,
when my brother's
    being nasty,
when a spider makes me scream,
when I stamp and lose my temper,
when I think nobody cares,
    who is there?
God is there!

When I see a baby puppy,
when my best friend comes to play,
when I wear my favourite T-shirt,
when I have a brilliant day,
when I hear a funny story,
when the sun shines bright and fair,
    who is there?
God is there!

Feeling sad

Flowers and pets and people die;
it makes me sad; it makes me cry.
Jesus, I'm glad to know you're near,
to comfort me and soothe my tears.

A young child may not yet realise that death is permanent and their grief may
come and go, in intense bursts. They need loving support to help them cope with
their very real feelings of loss and to answer their (often repeated) questions.

My busy day!

Hello Jesus.
I'm busy being busy –
being busy is such fun!

I'm busy going shopping,
and I love to go to town.
It's brilliant in the trolley,
as we trundle up and
      down.

I'm busy when I go
      to church,
we sing and then
      we pray,
I hear a Bible story,
and I make some things
      and play.

I'm busy being busy –
being busy is such fun!

While I sleep

All night long, while I sleep,
Jesus, I know that you will keep me
snug in your love, cosy in your care,
safe in your strength,
    'cause you're always there.

Goodnight, Jesus.

Feeling scared

Dear God,
I didn't like the pictures on television.
People were hurt and crying.
I'm scared.
Will it happen here?
Will it happen to me?

God says, 'Do not be afraid. I will be with you to help you wherever you go.'

(Joshua 1:9, paraphrased)

We cannot always protect children from bad news and negative images. But we can help them, by allowing them to talk about what they have seen and how they feel – and by not dismissing their worries.

You know me

Jesus,
you know me,
you know what I'm doing,
you know how I'm feeling,
and you care about me
all the time.

Good!

Never alone

If I'm lonely in the night,
if I have a nasty fright,
God is with me all the way.
God is with me every day.
I am never all alone.
With God, I'm never on my own.

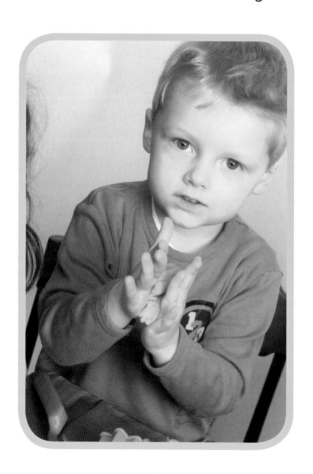

So much to tell you!

I've got so much to tell you, Jesus!

All about what I've done today...

all about my family...

all about my friends...

Did you have a busy day, like me?

This prayer gives a pattern for a child to talk about everything. You could use the prayer, together, at bedtime. After each line, tell Jesus all your news.

Look at me!

Look at me, Jesus!
I look so different with my hair like that
but inside, I'm still me.
I may look a scruff or I may look smart,
but I know it's ME you see.

Look at me, Jesus!
I look so different with my clothes like that
but inside, I'm still me.
I may look a scruff or I may look smart,
but I know it's ME you see.

Breaking friends

My friend says we're not friends any more.
I don't know why.
Please help us make friends again.

As adults, we know that children's friendships are often broken and re-made quickly. But, at the time, the child's feelings are strong and raw. Listen to their story and assure them of your love and care for them.

My own prayers

How do you feel today?
Tell God about it.

Sorry prayers

When we help our children understand what it means to be sorry and when we forgive them, we are helping them to learn what it means to be forgiven by God.

I'm sorry

Father God,
I'm sorry
for doing wrong.
Please forgive me.

Please help me
not to do it again.

Looking after God's world

Dear God, are you sad
 when you look at
 your world?
Does the mess that
 we've made make
 you sigh?
From the smallest sweet wrapper chucked
 down on the ground
to the ozone layer holes in the sky?

Help us to respect and take care
 of your world.
Teach us not to spoil or to waste;
to enjoy, not destroy, all the beauty we see
to keep your world a wonderful place.

Please help me

Father God,
  sometimes I get grumpy and cross –
I'm sorry.
Sometimes I don't want to share –
I'm sorry.
Sometimes I am horrid to my friends –
I'm sorry.
Sometimes I won't do
  as I'm asked –
I'm sorry.

Father God, I am sorry.
Thank you that
you love me.
Please help me
to start again.

A rotten day

It was a rotten day today,
and everyone got cross.
I spilled my drink down my new shirt,
and then one shoe got lost.

It was a rotten day today,
though God was always there,
but we were all so grumpy,
we'd forgotten that he cares.

But God did not forget us,
when we grumbled, whinged and moaned.
He helped us to be friends again
and happy in our home.

Feeling cross

I'm so cross, I'm going to burst!
I want to scream and shout and stamp
    and do my worst.

Help me God! I don't know how.
Help me come down,
    climb down,
        cool down,
            calm down,
                NOW.

Being sorry

Father God, I'm so sorry.

You do still love me, don't you?

God's answer:

"You are precious to me and I love you,
Do not be afraid – I am with you."

(paraphrased from Isaiah 43)

Please
prayers

For people who are not very well

Dear Jesus,
you made people
      better when they
      were poorly.
Please make (name) better today.
Thank you.

Feeling shy

People tell me, "Don't be shy!"
but I feel wobbly, inside.
Please Jesus, help me to be brave
when I want to run and hide.

People without homes

Father, it's sad that some people
    don't have homes;
sleeping out of doors, sheltering
    in cardboard boxes.
It must be so cold and uncomfy –
    and frightening too.
Please comfort and protect them
    and help them find homes soon.

Be with me

Dear Jesus, please be with me,
I like to know you care.
When everything is hard for me,
it's good to know you're there.
I'm glad you're close beside me, Lord,
a friend, to hold my hand.
I'm glad you know just how I feel —
you always understand.

Please help me

Dear God,
please help me to share,
please help me to care,
please help me be fair.

Help me to get better

Dear Jesus,
please help me to get better.
(I don't like being ill.)
Please help my doctor.
(I don't like taking medicine.)
Please help me feel like me again.
(Quickly!)

School day

Today is a school day,
a work day, a long day,
a learning, listening, play day.
Please be with me, today.

Today is a school day,
a words day, a paint day,
a numbers, spelling, sports day.
Please help me, Lord, today.

Help me to be good

When we go on a journey,
please help me to be good.
When we go round the shops,
please help me to be good.
When someone comes to call,
please help me to be good.
Jesus, any time and anywhere,
please help me to be good.

Being kind

Sharing, caring, being fair,
kind to others everywhere,
being loving, helping too –
that's what God wants me to do.

Please help me, God.

Happy times

Dear God,
Please make today a good day.
Please help me to be helpful.
Please show me how to be kind.
Please make me friendly,
so we all have a happy time together.
Thanks!

God's way

When I'm in my home,
    the place where I belong,
Jesus, help me know what's right or wrong.
Each and every day,
    please help me choose your way.

Holidays!

Dear Lord,
it's holiday time.
Please help us have fun
when we're out and about,
in the rain and the sun.
There's so much to do,
the time just zooms by.
Help our holiday days,
be a wonderful time.

Bedtime

Time for bed and time for sleep.
Mummy loves me and Daddy loves me.
My brother loves me
   and my sister loves me.
My family and my friends love me.
And, most of all, God loves me.
Please be with me tonight,
   my loving lovely God!

My own prayers

What do you want to ask God?

Special day
prayers

Going to church

The place where we meet,
the people we greet,
the songs that we sing,
the offering we bring,
the stories we hear,
the friends we sit near,
it's all done for you.
We're glad you're there too!

Parties

What's inside? I just can't wait!
Opening presents is really great.
Pull off the paper to see what's there –
a toy, some sweets or clothes to wear?
It's fun to know this gift is mine.
Thank you, God, for present-time.

Choosing a present for a special date –
Giving presents is really great.

Wrap round the paper
to hide what's there –
a toy, some sweets
or clothes to wear.
Giving a gift makes
me feel fine.
Thank you, God, for
present-time.

Our new baby

Our baby's fresh and new and floppy,
with wrinkly skin that doesn't fit,
with a baby smell and a baby cry,
and baby fingers with a mega grip.

Thank you for our baby,
for this wonderful birth-day
Thank you Lord for (name)
      HURRAY!

(Did I ever look like that?)

Going swimming

Guess where I've been, Jesus?

Somewhere where it
  tastes sharp,
    feels wet,
      smells clean,
        looks dazzly,
          sounds jangly...

SWIMMING!

I've had a wonderful time.
  Thanks!

Party fun

I love the tingle in my tum,
I feel I just can't wait,
I love to dress in party clothes,
a party is so great!

I love the noise, I love the games
with prizes to be won.
I love the food and fizzy drinks,
a party is such fun.

Thank you, God, for parties.

Harvest time

Sing a song of harvest,
sing a song today.
All the crops are gathered,
safely stored away.
Harvest, harvest,
God has given us harvest.
Thank you, God, for all the food
you give to us today.

Christmas Day

Happy birthday, Jesus!
Happy birthday to you,
happy birthday to you,
Today is your birthday –
and it's Christmas Day, too!

Want to help your child start to read the Bible? *Tiddlywinks: My Little Books* are designed for you to use together. Each page has a story and an appropriate passage from the Bible to help you start your child off on the journey of getting to know God through the Bible!

My Little Red Book Christmas and more...
9781859996591

My Little Blue Book You and more...
9781859996607

My Little Green Book Creation and more...
9781859996966

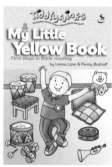

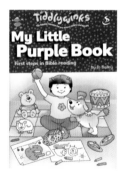

My little Yellow Book Easter and more...
9781859996935

My Little Purple Book Jesus and more...
9781859997208

My Little Orange Book The Bible and more...
9781859997178

All priced £3.50

Available from your local Christian bookshop, SU Mail Order (0845 07 06 006) or from www.scriptureunion.org.uk/shop. Prices correct at time of going to press.